Hidden in My Heart

Tena DeGraaf

WESTBOW
PRESS®
A DIVISION OF THOMAS NELSON
& ZONDERVAN

Copyright © 2016 Tena DeGraaf.
Monica Lee-Cover Illustration

All rights reserved. No part of this book may be used or reproduced by any means, graphic, electronic, or mechanical, including photocopying, recording, taping or by any information storage retrieval system without the written permission of the author except in the case of brief quotations embodied in critical articles and reviews.

This book is a work of non-fiction. Unless otherwise noted, the author and the publisher make no explicit guarantees as to the accuracy of the information contained in this book and in some cases, names of people and places have been altered to protect their privacy.

Scripture taken from the Holy Bible, NEW INTERNATIONAL VERSION®. Copyright © 1973, 1978, 1984, 2011 by Biblica, Inc. All rights reserved worldwide. Used by permission. NEW INTERNATIONAL VERSION® and NIV® are registered trademarks of Biblica, Inc. Use of either trademark for the offering of goods or services requires the prior written consent of Biblica US, Inc.

WestBow Press books may be ordered through booksellers or by contacting:

WestBow Press
A Division of Thomas Nelson & Zondervan
1663 Liberty Drive
Bloomington, IN 47403
www.westbowpress.com
1 (866) 928-1240

Because of the dynamic nature of the Internet, any web addresses or links contained in this book may have changed since publication and may no longer be valid. The views expressed in this work are solely those of the author and do not necessarily reflect the views of the publisher, and the publisher hereby disclaims any responsibility for them.

Any people depicted in stock imagery provided by Thinkstock are models, and such images are being used for illustrative purposes only.
Certain stock imagery © Thinkstock.

ISBN: 978-1-5127-2697-8 (sc)
ISBN: 978-1-5127-2699-2 (hc)
ISBN: 978-1-5127-2698-5 (e)

Library of Congress Control Number: 2016900407

Print information available on the last page.

WestBow Press rev. date: 3/3/2016

Acknowledgements

With special thanks to all my family members and friends who graciously shared with me the verses that they have hidden in their hearts.

Introduction

With our fast-paced lifestyles today, it is often a challenge to make time to read God's Word. *Hidden in My Heart* was designed to make the most of small fragments of time to reflect on verses of Scripture. You may keep this book on your nightstand, on the kitchen counter, or in your car. Regardless of where you read it, it will always remind you to meditate on a verse each day. There is an insightful daily verse beginning with Genesis in January and ending with Revelation in December. *Hidden in My Heart* walks you through the Bible day by day with at least one inspirational verse from each book of the Bible. This collection of daily Scriptures and accompanying space for personal journaling will enrich your daily walk with God by providing structure for your own reflection and meditation on God's Word. May this book become as meaningful to you as writing it has been to me. And may you always be aware of God's truths and His constant love for you.

Tena

January 1

In the beginning God created
the heavens and the earth.
Genesis 1:1

January 2

God saw all that he had made,
and it was very good.
Genesis 1:31

January 3

He rested from all his work.
Genesis 2:2

January 4

The LORD is my strength and my defense;
he has become my salvation.

Exodus 15:2

_____
_____
_____

January 5

For I am the LORD, who heals you.

Exodus 15:26

_____
_____
_____

January 6

You shall have no other gods before me.

Exodus 20:3

_____
_____
_____

January 7

You shall not make for yourself an image
in the form of anything in heaven above
or on the earth beneath or in the waters below.
Exodus 20:4

January 8

You shall not misuse the
name of the LORD your God.
Exodus 20:7

January 9

Remember the Sabbath day
by keeping it holy.
Exodus 20:8

January 10

Honor your father and your mother, so that you may live long in the land the LORD your God is giving you.
Exodus 20:12

January 11

You shall not murder.
Exodus 20:13

January 12

You shall not commit adultery.
Exodus 20:14

January 13

You shall not steal.
Exodus 20:15

_____
_____
_____

January 14

You shall not give false testimony
against your neighbor.
Exodus 20:16

_____
_____
_____

January 15

You shall not covet your neighbor's house...
or anything that belongs to your neighbor.
Exodus 20:17

_____
_____
_____

January 16

Love your neighbor as yourself.
Leviticus 19:18

_____
_____
_____

January 17

Show respect for the elderly
and revere your God.
Leviticus 19:32

_____
_____
_____

January 18

I will walk among you and be your God,
and you will be my people.
Leviticus 26:12

_____
_____
_____

January 19

The LORD bless you and keep you;
the LORD make his face shine on you
and be gracious to you; the LORD turn his
face toward you and give you peace.
Numbers 6:24–26

_____
_____
_____
_____

January 20

The LORD is slow to anger, abounding in
love and forgiving sin and rebellion.
Numbers 14:18

_____
_____
_____
_____

January 21

Only be careful, and watch yourselves closely
so that you do not forget the things your eyes have
seen or let them fade from your heart as long
as you live. Teach them to your children
and to their children after them.
Deuteronomy 4:9

_____
_____
_____
_____

January 22

We will listen and obey.
Deuteronomy 5:27

_____
_____
_____
_____

January 23

Love the LORD your God with
all your heart and with all your soul
and with all your strength.
Deuteronomy 6:5

_____
_____
_____
_____

January 24

These commandments that I give you today
are to be on your hearts.
Impress them on your children.
Talk about them when you sit at home
and when you walk along the road,
when you lie down and when you get up.
Deuteronomy 6:6–7

_____
_____
_____
_____

January 25

Fix these words of mine in your
hearts and minds.
Deuteronomy 11:18

January 26

Obey the LORD your God and
follow his commands.
Deuteronomy 27:10

January 27

The eternal God is your refuge,
and underneath are the everlasting arms.
Deuteronomy 33:27

January 28

I will never leave you nor forsake you.
Joshua 1:5

_____
_____
_____
_____

January 29

Keep this Book of the Law
always on your lips;
meditate on it day and night,
so that you may be careful
to do everything written in it.
Joshua 1:8

_____
_____
_____
_____

January 30

Be strong and courageous.
Do not be afraid; do not be discouraged,
for the LORD your God will be with you
wherever you go.
Joshua 1:9

_____
_____
_____
_____

January 31

You know with all your heart and soul
that not one of all the good promises
the LORD your God gave you has failed.
Every promise has been fulfilled;
not one has failed.
Joshua 23:14

_____
_____
_____
_____

February 1

But as for me and my household,
we will serve the LORD.
Joshua 24:15

February 2

I, even I, will sing to the LORD;
I will praise the LORD,
the God of Israel, in song.
Judges 5:3

February 3

May you be richly rewarded by the LORD,
the God of Israel,
under whose wings you have
come to take refuge.
Ruth 2:12

February 4

But be sure to fear the LORD
and serve him faithfully with all your heart;
consider what great things
he has done for you.
1 Samuel 12:24

February 5

To obey is better than sacrifice.
1 Samuel 15:22

February 6

The LORD does not look at the
things people look at.
People look at the outward appearance,
but the LORD looks at the heart.
1 Samuel 16:7

February 7

The LORD rewards everyone
for their righteousness and faithfulness.
1 Samuel 26:23

February 8

You, LORD, are my lamp;
the LORD turns my darkness into light.
2 Samuel 22:29

February 9

It is God who arms me with strength
and keeps my way secure.
2 Samuel 22:33

February 10

Therefore I will praise you, LORD,
among the nations;
I will sing the praises of your name.
2 Samuel 22:50

February 11

LORD, the God of Israel,
there is no God like you
in heaven above or on earth below.
1 Kings 8:23

February 12

And Elisha prayed,
"Open his eyes, LORD, so that he may see."
2 Kings 6:17

February 13

Look to the LORD and his strength;
seek his face always.
1 Chronicles 16:11

_____
_____
_____
_____

February 14

Give thanks to the LORD, for he is good;
his love endures forever.
1 Chronicles 16:34

_____
_____
_____
_____

February 15

For everything in heaven and earth is yours.
1 Chronicles 29:11

_____
_____
_____
_____

February 16

For the eyes of the LORD range throughout
the earth to strengthen those whose
hearts are fully committed to him.
2 Chronicles 16:9

February 17

For the LORD your God is
gracious and compassionate.
He will not turn his face from you
if you return to him.
2 Chronicles 30:9

February 18

The gracious hand of our God
is on everyone who looks to him,
but his great anger is against
all who forsake him.
Ezra 8:22

February 19

Do not grieve,
for the joy of the LORD is your strength.
Nehemiah 8:10

February 20

For if you remain silent at this time,
relief and deliverance for the Jews will
arise from another place,
but you and your father's family
will perish. And who knows but
that you have come to your royal
position for such a time as this?
Esther 4:14

February 21

Teach me, and I will be quiet;
show me where I have been wrong.
Job 6:24

February 22

I know that my redeemer lives.
Job 19:25

_____
_____
_____

February 23

The price of wisdom is beyond rubies.
Job 28:18

_____
_____
_____

February 24

The fear of the Lord–
that is wisdom,
and to shun evil is understanding.
Job 28:28

_____
_____
_____

February 25

Stop and consider God's wonders.
Job 37:14

February 26

Blessed is the one
who does not walk in step with
the wicked or stand in the way that sinners
take or sit in the company of mockers,
but whose delight is in the law of the LORD,
and who meditates on his law day and night.
Psalm 1:1–2

February 27

Tremble and do not sin.
Psalm 4:4

February 28

In peace I will lie down and sleep,
for you alone, LORD,
make me dwell in safety.

Psalm 4:8

_____
_____
_____

February 29

LORD, our Lord,
how majestic is your name in all the earth!

Psalm 8:9

_____
_____
_____

March 1

The LORD is my rock,
my fortress and my deliverer;
my God is my rock, in whom I take refuge,
my shield and the horn of my salvation,
my stronghold.

Psalm 18:2

March 2

The LORD is my shepherd,
I lack nothing.
He makes me lie down in green pastures,
he leads me beside quiet waters,
he refreshes my soul.
He guides me along the right paths
for his name's sake.
Even though I walk through
the darkest valley,
I will fear no evil, for you are with me;
your rod and your staff, they comfort me.

Psalm 23:1–4

March 3

Show me your ways,
LORD, teach me your paths.
Guide me in your truth and teach me.
Psalm 25:4–5

March 4

LORD my God,
I called to you for help, and you healed me.
Psalm 30:2

March 5

LORD my God,
I will praise you forever.
Psalm 30:12

March 6

You are my hiding place;
you will protect me from trouble
and surround me with songs of deliverance.
Psalm 32:7

March 7

The LORD loves righteousness and justice;
the earth is full of his unfailing love.
Psalm 33:5

March 8

I sought the LORD, and he answered me;
he delivered me from all my fears.
Psalm 34:4

March 9

Take delight in the LORD,
and he will give you the
desires of your heart.
Psalm 37:4

March 10

I desire to do your will, my God;
your law is within my heart.
Psalm 40:8

March 11

God is our refuge and strength,
an ever-present help in trouble.
Psalm 46:1

March 12

Be still, and know that I am God.
Psalm 46:10

_____
_____
_____
_____

March 13

Create in me a pure heart, O God,
and renew a steadfast spirit within me.
Do not cast me from your presence
or take your Holy Spirit from me.
Restore to me the joy of your salvation
and grant me a willing spirit, to sustain me.
Psalm 51:10–12

_____
_____
_____
_____

March 14

When I am afraid, I put my trust in you.
Psalm 56:3

_____
_____
_____
_____

March 15

Truly my soul finds rest in God.
Psalm 62:1

March 16

You, God, are my God,
earnestly I seek you.
Psalm 63:1

March 17

Praise be to God,
who has not rejected my prayer
or withheld his love from me!
Psalm 66:20

March 18

Praise be to the Lord, to God our Savior,
who daily bears our burdens.
Psalm 68:19

March 19

Better is one day in your courts
than a thousand elsewhere;
I would rather be a doorkeeper
in the house of my God
than dwell in the tents of the wicked.
Psalm 84:10

March 20

Teach me your way, LORD,
that I may rely on your faithfulness.
Psalm 86:11

March 21

Teach us to number our days,
that we may gain a heart of wisdom.
Psalm 90:12

_____
_____
_____

March 22

Whoever dwells in the shelter of the Most High
will rest in the shadow of the Almighty.
Psalm 91:1

_____
_____
_____

March 23

As far as the east is from the west,
so far has he removed our transgressions from us.
Psalm 103:12

_____
_____
_____

March 24

The LORD has done it this very day;
let us rejoice today and be glad.
Psalm 118:24

March 25

Blessed are those who keep his statutes
and seek him with all their heart.
Psalm 119:2

March 26

I have hidden your word in my heart
that I might not sin against you.
Psalm 119:11

March 27

Turn my eyes away from worthless things.
Psalm 119:37

March 28

Oh, how I love your law!
I meditate on it all day long.
Psalm 119:97

March 29

Your word is a lamp for my feet,
a light on my path.
Psalm 119:105

March 30

Great peace have those who love your law,
and nothing can make them stumble.
Psalm 119:165

_____
_____
_____
_____

March 31

Unless the LORD builds the house,
the builders labor in vain.
Psalm 127:1

_____
_____
_____
_____

April 1

Search me, God, and know my heart;
test me and know my anxious thoughts.
See if there is any offensive way in me,
and lead me in the way everlasting.
Psalm 139:23–24

April 2

Set a guard over my mouth, LORD;
keep watch over the door of my lips.
Psalm 141:3

April 3

Teach me to do your will,
for you are my God.
Psalm 143:10

April 4

The LORD is near to all who call on him,
to all who call on him in truth.

Psalm 145:18

April 5

The LORD delights in those who fear him,
who put their hope in his unfailing love.

Psalm 147:11

April 6

Let everything that has breath
praise the LORD.

Psalm 150:6

April 7

Trust in the LORD with all your heart
and lean not on your own understanding;
in all your ways submit to him,
and he will make your paths straight.
Proverbs 3:5–6

_____
_____
_____

April 8

My son, pay attention to what I say;
turn your ear to my words.
Proverbs 4:20

_____
_____
_____

April 9

Above all else, guard your heart,
for everything you do flows from it.
Proverbs 4:23

_____
_____
_____

April 10

I love those who love me,
and those who seek me find me.

Proverbs 8:17

_____
_____
_____
_____

April 11

Blessed is the one who is kind to the needy.

Proverbs 14:21

_____
_____
_____
_____

April 12

Commit to the LORD whatever you do,
and he will establish your plans.

Proverbs 16:3

_____
_____
_____
_____

April 13

Gracious words are a honeycomb,
sweet to the soul and healing to the bones.
Proverbs 16:24

_____
_____
_____

April 14

A friend loves at all times.
Proverbs 17:17

_____
_____
_____

April 15

A cheerful heart is good medicine.
Proverbs 17:22

_____
_____
_____

April 16

The name of the LORD is a fortified tower;
the righteous run to it and are safe.
Proverbs 18:10

April 17

There is a friend who
sticks closer than a brother.
Proverbs 18:24

April 18

Ears that hear and eyes that see—
the LORD has made them both.
Proverbs 20:12

April 19

Start children off on the way they should go,
and even when they are old they will not turn from it.
Proverbs 22:6

April 20

Pay attention and turn your ear
to the sayings of the wise;
apply your heart to what I teach.
Proverbs 22:17

April 21

For it is pleasing when you
keep them in your heart
and have all of them ready on your lips.
Proverbs 22:18

April 22

As iron sharpens iron,
so one person sharpens another.
Proverbs 27:17

_____
_____
_____
_____

April 23

There is a time for everything,
and a season for every
activity under the heavens.
Ecclesiastes 3:1

_____
_____
_____
_____

April 24

He has made everything
beautiful in its time.
Ecclesiastes 3:11

_____
_____
_____
_____

April 25

If either of them falls down,
one can help the other up.
Ecclesiastes 4:10

_____
_____
_____

April 26

When times are good, be happy.
Ecclesiastes 7:14

_____
_____
_____

April 27

Many waters cannot quench love;
rivers cannot sweep it away.
Song of Songs 8:7

_____
_____
_____

April 28

Though your sins are like scarlet,
they shall be as white as snow;
though they are red as crimson,
they shall be like wool.
Isaiah 1:18

April 29

For to us a child is born,
to us a son is given, and the government
will be on his shoulders. And he will be
called Wonderful Counselor, Mighty God,
Everlasting Father, Prince of Peace.
Isaiah 9:6

April 30

You will keep in perfect peace those whose minds
are steadfast, because they trust in you.
Isaiah 26:3

May 1

For the LORD is a God of justice.
Blessed are all who wait for him!
Isaiah 30:18

May 2

The grass withers and the flowers fall,
but the word of our God endures forever.
Isaiah 40:8

May 3

He tends his flock like a shepherd:
He gathers the lambs in his arms
and carries them close to his heart;
he gently leads those that have young.
Isaiah 40:11

May 4

Do you not know? Have you not heard?
The LORD is the everlasting God,
the Creator of the ends of the earth.
He will not grow tired or weary,
and his understanding no one can fathom.
Isaiah 40:28

May 5

But those who hope in the LORD will renew their strength. They will soar on wings like eagles; they will run and not grow weary, they will walk and not be faint.
Isaiah 40:31

May 6

So do not fear, for I am with you;
do not be dismayed, for I am your God.
I will strengthen you and help you;
I will uphold you with my righteous right hand.
Isaiah 41:10

_____
_____
_____

May 7

Forget the former things; do not dwell on the past.
Isaiah 43:18

_____
_____
_____

May 8

The Sovereign LORD has given me a well-instructed tongue,
to know the word that sustains the weary.
He wakens me morning by morning,
wakens my ear to listen like one being instructed.
Isaiah 50:4

_____
_____
_____

May 9

But he was pierced for our transgressions,
he was crushed for our iniquities;
the punishment that brought
us peace was on him,
and by his wounds we are healed.
Isaiah 53:5

_____
_____
_____

May 10

So is my word that goes out from my mouth:
It will not return to me empty,
but will accomplish what I desire
and achieve the purpose for which I sent it.
Isaiah 55:11

_____
_____
_____

May 11

The LORD will guide you always.
Isaiah 58:11

_____
_____
_____

May 12

I will tell of the kindnesses of the LORD,
the deeds for which he is to be praised.
Isaiah 63:7

May 13

Yet you, LORD, are our Father.
We are the clay, you are the potter;
we are all the work of your hand.
Isaiah 64:8

May 14

Before they call I will answer;
while they are still speaking I will hear.
Isaiah 65:24

May 15

As a mother comforts her child,
so will I comfort you.
Isaiah 66:13

_____
_____
_____
_____

May 16

Ask where the good way is, and walk in it,
and you will find rest for your souls.
Jeremiah 6:16

_____
_____
_____
_____

May 17

But blessed is the one who trusts in the LORD,
whose confidence is in him.
Jeremiah 17:7

_____
_____
_____
_____

May 18

Heal me, LORD, and I will be healed;
save me and I will be saved,
for you are the one I praise.
Jeremiah 17:14

_____
_____
_____

May 19

"For I know the plans I have for you,"
declares the LORD,
"plans to prosper you and not to harm you,
plans to give you hope and a future."
Jeremiah 29:11

_____
_____
_____

May 20

You will seek me and find me
when you seek me with all your heart.
Jeremiah 29:13

_____
_____
_____

May 21

I have loved you with an everlasting love;
I have drawn you with unfailing kindness.
Jeremiah 31:3

May 22

I will turn their mourning into gladness;
I will give them comfort and joy
instead of sorrow.
Jeremiah 31:13

May 23

I will refresh the weary and satisfy the faint.
Jeremiah 31:25

May 24

I am the LORD, the God of all mankind.
Is anything too hard for me?
Jeremiah 32:27

May 25

Call to me and I will answer you
and tell you great and unsearchable things
you do not know.
Jeremiah 33:3

May 26

The LORD is good to those
whose hope is in him,
to the one who seeks him.
Lamentations 3:25

May 27

It is good to wait quietly
for the salvation of the LORD.
Lamentations 3:26

May 28

Let us examine our ways and test them,
and let us return to the LORD.
Lamentations 3:40

May 29

There will be showers of blessing.
Ezekiel 34:26

May 30

I will give you a new heart and
put a new spirit in you;
I will remove from you your heart of stone
and give you a heart of flesh.
Ezekiel 36:26

May 31

How great are his signs,
how mighty his wonders!
His kingdom is an eternal kingdom;
his dominion endures from
generation to generation.
Daniel 4:3

June 1

Those who are wise
will shine like the brightness of the heavens,
and those who lead many to righteousness,
like the stars for ever and ever.

Daniel 12:3

June 2

Let us acknowledge the LORD;
let us press on to acknowledge him.

Hosea 6:3

June 3

Forgive all our sins
and receive us graciously.

Hosea 14:2

June 4

Mighty is the army that obeys his command.
Joel 2:11

June 5

Return to the LORD your God,
for he is gracious and compassionate,
slow to anger and abounding in love.
Joel 2:13

June 6

Seek good, not evil,
that you may live.
Amos 5:14

June 7

Sovereign LORD, forgive!
Amos 7:2

_____
_____
_____

June 8

The day of the LORD is near for all nations.
As you have done, it will be done to you;
your deeds will return upon your own head.
Obadiah 1:15

_____
_____
_____

June 9

Salvation comes from the LORD.
Jonah 2:9

_____
_____
_____

June 10

And what does the LORD require of you?
To act justly and to love mercy
and to walk humbly with your God.
Micah 6:8

June 11

But as for me, I watch in hope for the LORD,
I wait for God my Savior;
my God will hear me.
Micah 7:7

June 12

The LORD is good,
a refuge in times of trouble.
He cares for those who trust in him.
Nahum 1:7

June 13

Yet I will rejoice in the LORD,
I will be joyful in God my Savior.
Habakkuk 3:18

June 14

The Sovereign LORD is my strength.
Habakkuk 3:19

June 15

The LORD your God is with you,
the Mighty Warrior who saves.
He will take great delight in you;
in his love he will no longer rebuke you,
but will rejoice over you with singing.
Zephaniah 3:17

June 16

From this day on I will bless you.
Haggai 2:19

June 17

"Return to me," declares the LORD Almighty,
"and I will return to you."
Zechariah 1:3

June 18

"Not by might nor by power, but by my Spirit,"
says the LORD Almighty.
Zechariah 4:6

June 19

This is what the LORD Almighty said:
"Administer true justice;
show mercy and compassion to one another.
Do not oppress the widow
or the fatherless, the foreigner or the poor.
Do not plot evil against each other."
Zechariah 7:9–10

_____
_____
_____
_____

June 20

Do we not all have one Father?
Did not one God create us?
Malachi 2:10

_____
_____
_____
_____

June 21

I the LORD do not change.
Malachi 3:6

_____
_____
_____
_____

June 22

They will call him Immanuel
(which means "God with us").
Matthew 1:23

June 23

Man shall not live on bread alone,
but on every word that
comes from the mouth of God.
Matthew 4:4

June 24

Worship the Lord your God,
and serve him only.
Matthew 4:10

June 25

"Come, follow me," Jesus said,
"and I will send you out to fish for people."
Matthew 4:19

_____
_____
_____
_____

June 26

Blessed are the poor in spirit,
for theirs is the kingdom of heaven.
Matthew 5:3

_____
_____
_____
_____

June 27

Blessed are those who mourn,
for they will be comforted.
Matthew 5:4

_____
_____
_____
_____

June 28

Blessed are the meek,
for they will inherit the earth.
Matthew 5:5

June 29

Blessed are those who hunger and thirst
for righteousness,
for they will be filled.
Matthew 5:6

June 30

Blessed are the merciful,
for they will be shown mercy.
Matthew 5:7

July 1

Blessed are the pure in heart,
for they will see God.
Matthew 5:8

_____
_____
_____
_____

July 2

Blessed are the peacemakers,
for they will be called children of God.
Matthew 5:9

_____
_____
_____
_____

July 3

Blessed are those who are persecuted
because of righteousness,
for theirs is the kingdom of heaven.
Matthew 5:10

_____
_____
_____
_____

July 4

Blessed are you when people insult you,
persecute you and falsely say all kinds of
evil against you because of me.
Rejoice and be glad, because great is your
reward in heaven, for in the same way they
persecuted the prophets who were before you.
Matthew 5:11–12

July 5

In the same way,
let your light shine before others,
that they may see your good deeds
and glorify your Father in heaven.
Matthew 5:16

July 6

This, then, is how you should pray:
"Our Father in heaven,
hallowed be your name,
your kingdom come,
your will be done,
on earth as it is in heaven.
Give us today our daily bread.
And forgive us our debts,
as we also have forgiven our debtors.
And lead us not into temptation,
but deliver us from the evil one."
Matthew 6:9–13

July 7

Do not store up for yourselves treasures
on earth, where moths and vermin destroy,
and where thieves break in and steal.
Matthew 6:19

July 8

But store up for yourselves treasures in
heaven, where moths and vermin do not destroy,
and where thieves do not break in and steal.
Matthew 6:20

July 9

For where your treasure is,
there your heart will be also.
Matthew 6:21

July 10

You cannot serve both God and money.
Matthew 6:24

July 11

But seek first his kingdom and his righteousness,
and all these things will be given to you as well.
Matthew 6:33

_____
_____
_____
_____

July 12

Therefore do not worry about tomorrow,
for tomorrow will worry about itself.
Matthew 6:34

_____
_____
_____
_____

July 13

Ask and it will be given to you;
seek and you will find;
knock and the door will be opened to you.
For everyone who asks receives;
the one who seeks finds; and to the one who knocks,
the door will be opened.
Matthew 7:7–8

_____
_____
_____
_____

July 14

Come to me,
all you who are weary and burdened,
and I will give you rest.
Matthew 11:28

July 15

For where two or three gather
in my name, there am I with them.
Matthew 18:20

July 16

With God all things are possible.
Matthew 19:26

July 17

Jesus replied:
"'Love the Lord your God
with all your heart and with all your soul
and with all your mind.'
This is the first and greatest
commandment. And the second is like it:
'Love your neighbor as yourself.'"
Matthew 22:37–39

July 18

Heaven and earth will pass away,
but my words will never pass away.
Matthew 24:35

July 19

Therefore go and make disciples of all nations,
baptizing them in the name of the Father
and of the Son and of the Holy Spirit.
Matthew 28:19

July 20

And surely I am with you always,
to the very end of the age.
Matthew 28:20

July 21

Let the little children come to me,
and do not hinder them,
for the kingdom of God
belongs to such as these.
Mark 10:14

July 22

Whatever you ask for in prayer,
believe that you have received it,
and it will be yours.

Mark 11:24

July 23

Go into all the world
and preach the gospel to all creation.

Mark 16:15

July 24

You will conceive and give birth to a son,
and you are to call him Jesus.

Luke 1:31

July 25

For the Mighty One has done
great things for me—
holy is his name.
Luke 1:49

July 26

Today in the town of David
a Savior has been born to you;
he is the Messiah, the Lord.
Luke 2:11

July 27

Glory to God in the highest heaven,
and on earth peace to those
on whom his favor rests.
Luke 2:14

July 28

Do to others as you would
have them do to you.
Luke 6:31

_____
_____
_____
_____

July 29

Do not judge, and you will not be judged.
Do not condemn,
and you will not be condemned.
Forgive, and you will be forgiven.
Luke 6:37

_____
_____
_____
_____

July 30

A good man brings good things
out of the good stored up in his heart,
and an evil man brings evil things
out of the evil stored up in his heart.
For the mouth speaks what the heart is full of.
Luke 6:45

_____
_____
_____
_____

July 31

I have given you authority
to trample on snakes and scorpions
and to overcome all the power of the enemy;
nothing will harm you.
Luke 10:19

_____
_____
_____

August 1

Father, if you are willing,
take this cup from me;
yet not my will, but yours be done.
Luke 22:42

August 2

Through him all things were made;
without him nothing was made
that has been made.
John 1:3

August 3

Jesus replied,
"Very truly I tell you,
no one can see the kingdom of God
unless they are born again."
John 3:3

August 4

For God so loved the world
that he gave his one and only Son, that
whoever believes in him shall not perish
but have eternal life.
John 3:16

_____
_____
_____
_____

August 5

When Jesus spoke again to the people, he said,
"I am the light of the world.
Whoever follows me
will never walk in darkness,
but will have the light of life."
John 8:12

_____
_____
_____
_____

August 6

Then you will know the truth,
and the truth will set you free.
John 8:32

_____
_____
_____
_____

August 7

The thief comes only to steal and kill and destroy;
I have come that they may have life,
and have it to the full.
John 10:10

August 8

I give them eternal life,
and they shall never perish;
no one will snatch them out of my hand.
John 10:28

August 9

You believe in God;
believe also in me.
John 14:1

August 10

Jesus answered,
"I am the way and the truth and the life.
No one comes to the Father except through me."
John 14:6

_____
_____
_____

August 11

If you love me, keep my commands.
John 14:15

_____
_____
_____

August 12

Whoever has my commands and keeps them
is the one who loves me.
The one who loves me will be loved by my Father,
and I too will love them and show myself to them.
John 14:21

_____
_____
_____

August 13

Jesus replied,
"Anyone who loves me will obey my teaching."
John 14:23

_____
_____
_____
_____

August 14

But the Advocate, the Holy Spirit,
whom the Father will send in my name,
will teach you all things
and will remind you of everything
I have said to you.
John 14:26

_____
_____
_____
_____

August 15

Peace I leave with you; my peace I give you.
John 14:27

_____
_____
_____
_____

August 16

I am the vine; you are the branches.
If you remain in me and I in you,
you will bear much fruit;
apart from me you can do nothing.
John 15:5

_____
_____
_____

August 17

If you remain in me and
my words remain in you,
ask whatever you wish,
and it will be done for you.
John 15:7

_____
_____
_____

August 18

My command is this:
Love each other as I have loved you.
John 15:12

_____
_____
_____

August 19

Very truly I tell you,
my Father will give you
whatever you ask in my name.
John 16:23

_____
_____
_____
_____

August 20

In this world you will have trouble.
But take heart! I have overcome the world.
John 16:33

_____
_____
_____
_____

August 21

Your word is truth.
John 17:17

_____
_____
_____
_____

August 22

But you will receive power
when the Holy Spirit comes on you;
and you will be my witnesses in Jerusalem,
and in all Judea and Samaria,
and to the ends of the earth.
Acts 1:8

_____
_____
_____
_____

August 23

Repent, then, and turn to God,
so that your sins may be wiped out, that
times of refreshing may come from the Lord.
Acts 3:19

_____
_____
_____
_____

August 24

Salvation is found in no one else,
for there is no other name under heaven
given to mankind by which we must be saved.
Acts 4:12

_____
_____
_____
_____

August 25

Peter and the other apostles replied:
"We must obey God rather than human beings!"
Acts 5:29

August 26

Believe in the Lord Jesus, and you will be saved.
Acts 16:31

August 27

For in him we live and move and have our being.
Acts 17:28

August 28

It is more blessed to give than to receive.
Acts 20:35

August 29

For I am not ashamed of the gospel,
because it is the power of God that brings
salvation to everyone who believes.
Romans 1:16

August 30

For all have sinned and
fall short of the glory of God.
Romans 3:23

August 31

But God demonstrates his own love
for us in this:
While we were still sinners,
Christ died for us.
Romans 5:8

_____
_____
_____
_____

September 1

For the wages of sin is death,
but the gift of God is eternal life
in Christ Jesus our Lord.
Romans 6:23

September 2

The mind governed by the flesh is death,
but the mind governed by the Spirit
is life and peace.
Romans 8:6

September 3

In the same way,
the Spirit helps us in our weakness.
We do not know what we ought to pray for,
but the Spirit himself intercedes for us through
wordless groans.
Romans 8:26

September 4

And we know that in all things
God works for the good of those who love him,
who have been called according to his purpose.
Romans 8:28

September 5

If God is for us, who can be against us?
Romans 8:31

September 6

Neither height nor depth,
nor anything else in all creation,
will be able to separate us
from the love of God that is in
Christ Jesus our Lord.
Romans 8:39

September 7

If you declare with your mouth,
"Jesus is Lord," and believe
in your heart that God raised him
from the dead, you will be saved.
For it is with your heart that you believe
and are justified, and it is with your mouth
that you profess your faith and are saved.
Romans 10:9–10

September 8

Do not conform to the pattern of this world, but be
transformed by the renewing of your mind.
Then you will be able to test
and approve what God's will is–
his good, pleasing and perfect will.
Romans 12:2

September 9

Be devoted to one another in love.
Honor one another above yourselves.
Romans 12:10

September 10

If your enemy is hungry, feed him;
if he is thirsty, give him something to drink.
Romans 12:20

September 11

For everything that was written in the past
was written to teach us,
so that through the endurance
taught in the Scriptures and the encouragement
they provide we might have hope.
Romans 15:4

September 12

Accept one another, then,
just as Christ accepted you,
in order to bring praise to God.
Romans 15:7

September 13

May the God of hope fill you with all joy
and peace as you trust in him, so
that you may overflow with hope
by the power of the Holy Spirit.
Romans 15:13

September 14

"What no eye has seen,
what no ear has heard,
and what no human mind has conceived"–
the things God has prepared for those who love him.
1 Corinthians 2:9

September 15

But each of you has your own gift from God;
one has this gift, another has that.
1 Corinthians 7:7

September 16

And God is faithful;
he will not let you be tempted
beyond what you can bear.
1 Corinthians 10:13

September 17

"I have the right to do anything," you say—
but not everything is beneficial.
"I have the right to do anything"—
but not everything is constructive.
No one should seek their own good,
but the good of others.
1 Corinthians 10:23–24

September 18

So whether you eat or drink or whatever you do,
do it all for the glory of God.
1 Corinthians 10:31

September 19

Love is patient, love is kind.
It does not envy, it does not boast, it is not proud.
It does not dishonor others, it is not self-seeking,
it is not easily angered, it keeps no record of wrongs.
1 Corinthians 13:4–5

September 20

Love does not delight in evil
but rejoices with the truth.
It always protects, always trusts,
always hopes, always perseveres.
Love never fails.
1 Corinthians 13:6–8

September 21

For what I received
I passed on to you as of first importance:
that Christ died for our sins
according to the Scriptures,
that he was buried,
that he was raised on the third day
according to the Scriptures.
1 Corinthians 15:3–4

September 22

"Where, O death, is your victory?
Where, O death, is your sting?"
1 Corinthians 15:55

September 23

Do everything in love.
1 Corinthians 16:14

September 24

We are hard pressed on every side,
but not crushed;
perplexed, but not in despair;
persecuted, but not abandoned;
struck down, but not destroyed.
2 Corinthians 4:8–9

September 25

So we fix our eyes not on what is seen,
but on what is unseen, since
what is seen is temporary,
but what is unseen is eternal.
2 Corinthians 4:18

September 26

For we live by faith, not by sight.
2 Corinthians 5:7

September 27

Therefore, if anyone is in Christ,
the new creation has come:
The old has gone, the new is here!
2 Corinthians 5:17

_____
_____
_____

September 28

God loves a cheerful giver.
2 Corinthians 9:7

_____
_____
_____

September 29

But he said to me,
"My grace is sufficient for you,
for my power is made perfect in weakness."
Therefore I will boast all the more gladly
about my weaknesses, so that
Christ's power may rest on me.
2 Corinthians 12:9

_____
_____
_____

September 30

That is why, for Christ's sake,
I delight in weaknesses, in insults,
in hardships, in persecutions, in difficulties.
For when I am weak, then I am strong.
2 Corinthians 12:10

October 1

I have been crucified with Christ
and I no longer live,
but Christ lives in me.
The life I now live in the body,
I live by faith in the Son of God,
who loved me and gave himself for me.
Galatians 2:20

October 2

Serve one another humbly in love.
Galatians 5:13

October 3

But the fruit of the Spirit is love,
joy, peace, forbearance, kindness,
goodness, faithfulness, gentleness
and self-control.
Galatians 5:22–23

October 4

Carry each other's burdens.
Galatians 6:2

October 5

Do not be deceived:
God cannot be mocked.
A man reaps what he sows.
Galatians 6:7

October 6

Whoever sows to please their flesh,
from the flesh will reap destruction;
whoever sows to please the Spirit,
from the Spirit will reap eternal life.
Galatians 6:8

October 7

Let us not become weary in doing good,
for at the proper time we will reap a
harvest if we do not give up.
Galatians 6:9

October 8

For it is by grace you have been saved, through faith–
and this is not from yourselves, it is the gift of God–
not by works, so that no one can boast.
Ephesians 2:8–9

October 9

For he himself is our peace.
Ephesians 2:14

October 10

"In your anger do not sin":
Do not let the sun go down
while you are still angry,
and do not give the devil a foothold.
Ephesians 4:26–27

October 11

Be kind and compassionate to one another,
forgiving each other,
just as in Christ God forgave you.
Ephesians 4:32

October 12

Follow God's example.
Ephesians 5:1

October 13

Children, obey your parents in the Lord,
for this is right.
Ephesians 6:1

October 14

Finally, be strong in the Lord
and in his mighty power.
Ephesians 6:10

October 15

Put on the full armor of God,
so that you can take your stand
against the devil's schemes.
Ephesians 6:11

October 16

And pray in the Spirit on all occasions
with all kinds of prayers and requests.
With this in mind, be alert and
always keep on praying for all the Lord's people.
Ephesians 6:18

October 17

Being confident of this,
that he who began a good work in you
will carry it on to completion
until the day of Christ Jesus.
Philippians 1:6

October 18

In your relationships with one another,
have the same mindset as Christ Jesus.
Philippians 2:5

October 19

For it is God who works in you to will
and to act in order to fulfill his good purpose.
Philippians 2:13

_____
_____
_____
_____

October 20

Do everything without grumbling or arguing.
Philippians 2:14

_____
_____
_____
_____

October 21

I want to know Christ—
yes, to know the power of his resurrection
and participation in his sufferings,
becoming like him in his death.
Philippians 3:10

_____
_____
_____

October 22

I press on toward the goal to win the prize
for which God has called me heavenward
in Christ Jesus.
Philippians 3:14

October 23

Rejoice in the Lord always.
I will say it again: Rejoice!
Philippians 4:4

October 24

Let your gentleness be evident to all.
Philippians 4:5

October 25

Do not be anxious about anything,
but in every situation, by prayer and petition,
with thanksgiving, present your requests to God.
Philippians 4:6

October 26

And the peace of God, which transcends all
understanding, will guard your hearts
and your minds in Christ Jesus.
Philippians 4:7

October 27

Whatever is true, whatever is noble,
whatever is right, whatever is pure,
whatever is lovely, whatever is admirable—
if anything is excellent or praiseworthy—
think about such things.
Philippians 4:8

October 28

For I have learned to be content
whatever the circumstances.
Philippians 4:11

October 29

I can do all this through
him who gives me strength.
Philippians 4:13

October 30

And my God will meet all your needs
according to the riches of his glory
in Christ Jesus.
Philippians 4:19

October 31

For in him all things were created:
things in heaven and on earth,
visible and invisible.
Colossians 1:16

_____
_____
_____
_____

November 1

Set your minds on things above,
not on earthly things.
Colossians 3:2

November 2

Forgive as the Lord forgave you.
Colossians 3:13

November 3

Let the message of Christ dwell among you richly.
Colossians 3:16

November 4

Whatever you do,
work at it with all your heart,
as working for the Lord, not for human masters.
Colossians 3:23

November 5

Devote yourselves to prayer,
being watchful and thankful.
Colossians 4:2

November 6

Let your conversation be
always full of grace, seasoned with salt,
so that you may know
how to answer everyone.
Colossians 4:6

November 7

For we believe that Jesus died and rose again.
1 Thessalonians 4:14

November 8

Therefore encourage one another
and build each other up,
just as in fact you are doing.
1 Thessalonians 5:11

November 9

Rejoice always, pray continually,
give thanks in all circumstances;
for this is God's will for you in Christ Jesus.
1 Thessalonians 5:16–18

November 10

Reject every kind of evil.
1 Thessalonians 5:22

November 11

Stand firm and hold fast to the teachings we passed on to you.
2 Thessalonians 2:15

November 12

Here is a trustworthy saying that deserves full acceptance: Christ Jesus came into the world to save sinners.
1 Timothy 1:15

November 13

For the love of money is
a root of all kinds of evil.
1 Timothy 6:10

November 14

And the Lord's servant must not be quarrelsome
but must be kind to everyone,
able to teach, not resentful.
2 Timothy 2:24

November 15

All Scripture is God-breathed
and is useful for teaching, rebuking,
correcting and training in righteousness,
so that the servant of God
may be thoroughly equipped
for every good work.
2 Timothy 3:16–17

November 16

Remind the people to be subject
to rulers and authorities, to be obedient,
to be ready to do whatever is good.

Titus 3:1

_____
_____
_____

November 17

I pray that your partnership with us in the faith
may be effective in deepening your understanding
of every good thing we share for the sake of Christ.

Philemon 1:6

_____
_____
_____

November 18

Your love has given me
great joy and encouragement.

Philemon 1:7

_____
_____
_____

November 19

For the word of God is alive and active.
Sharper than any double-edged sword,
it penetrates even to dividing soul
and spirit, joints and marrow; it judges the
thoughts and attitudes of the heart.
Hebrews 4:12

_____
_____
_____
_____

November 20

Let us then approach God's throne
of grace with confidence, so that we
may receive mercy and find grace to help
us in our time of need.
Hebrews 4:16

_____
_____
_____
_____

November 21

Now faith is confidence in what we hope for
and assurance about what we do not see.
Hebrews 11:1

_____
_____
_____
_____

November 22

And without faith it is impossible to please God,
because anyone who comes to him
must believe that he exists
and that he rewards those who earnestly seek him.

Hebrews 11:6

November 23

Let us throw off everything that hinders
and the sin that so easily entangles.
And let us run with perseverance
the race marked out for us.

Hebrews 12:1

November 24

Fixing our eyes on Jesus,
the pioneer and perfecter of faith.

Hebrews 12:2

November 25

Make every effort to live in peace with everyone
and to be holy.
Hebrews 12:14

November 26

Be content with what you have,
because God has said,
"Never will I leave you; never will I forsake you."
So we say with confidence,
"The Lord is my helper; I will not be afraid.
What can mere mortals do to me?"
Hebrews 13:5–6

November 27

Jesus Christ is the same
yesterday and today and forever.
Hebrews 13:8

November 28

And do not forget to do good
and to share with others, for with
such sacrifices God is pleased.

Hebrews 13:16

_____
_____
_____
_____

November 29

Consider it pure joy, my brothers and sisters,
whenever you face trials of many kinds,
because you know that the testing of your faith
produces perseverance.

James 1:2–3

_____
_____
_____
_____

November 30

If any of you lacks wisdom, you should ask God,
who gives generously to all without finding
fault, and it will be given to you.

James 1:5

_____
_____
_____
_____

December 1

Every good and perfect gift is from above,
coming down from the Father of the heavenly
lights, who does not change like shifting shadows.
James 1:17

December 2

Everyone should be quick to listen,
slow to speak and slow to become angry.
James 1:19

December 3

Do not merely listen to the word,
and so deceive yourselves.
Do what it says.
James 1:22

December 4

My brothers and sisters,
believers in our glorious Lord Jesus Christ
must not show favoritism.

James 2:1

_____
_____
_____
_____

December 5

If anyone, then, knows the good
they ought to do and doesn't do it, it is sin for them.

James 4:17

_____
_____
_____
_____

December 6

Is anyone among you in trouble? Let them pray.
Is anyone happy?
Let them sing songs of praise.

James 5:13

_____
_____
_____
_____

December 7

The prayer of a righteous person is
powerful and effective.
James 5:16

December 8

For it is written: "Be holy, because I am holy."
1 Peter 1:16

December 9

Finally, all of you, be like-minded,
be sympathetic, love one another,
be compassionate and humble.
1 Peter 3:8

December 10

Do not repay evil with evil or
insult with insult. On the contrary, repay evil
with blessing, because to this you were called
so that you may inherit a blessing.

1 Peter 3:9

_____
_____
_____
_____

December 11

But in your hearts revere Christ as Lord.
Always be prepared to give an answer to everyone
who asks you to give the reason for the hope that you have.
But do this with gentleness and respect.

1 Peter 3:15

_____
_____
_____
_____

December 12

Above all, love each other deeply,
because love covers over a multitude of sins.

1 Peter 4:8

_____
_____
_____
_____

December 13

Each of you should use whatever gift
you have received to serve others.
1 Peter 4:10

December 14

If anyone speaks, they should do so as one
who speaks the very words of God.
If anyone serves, they should do so with
the strength God provides,
so that in all things God may be
praised through Jesus Christ.
1 Peter 4:11

December 15

Cast all your anxiety on him
because he cares for you.
1 Peter 5:7

December 16

His divine power has given us everything
we need for a godly life.
2 Peter 1:3

December 17

God is light; in him there is no darkness at all.
1 John 1:5

December 18

If we confess our sins,
he is faithful and just
and will forgive us our sins
and purify us from all unrighteousness.
1 John 1:9

December 19

This is how we know what love is:
Jesus Christ laid down his life for us.
And we ought to lay down
our lives for our brothers and sisters.
1 John 3:16

December 20

Dear children,
let us not love with words or speech
but with actions and in truth.
1 John 3:18

December 21

Dear friends,
let us love one another,
for love comes from God.
1 John 4:7

December 22

God is love.
1 John 4:16

December 23

We love because he first loved us.
1 John 4:19

December 24

And this is the testimony:
God has given us eternal life,
and this life is in his Son.
Whoever has the Son has life;
whoever does not have the
Son of God does not have life.
1 John 5:11–12

December 25

And this is love:
that we walk in obedience to his commands.
As you have heard from the beginning,
his command is that you walk in love.
2 John 1:6

December 26

Dear friend, I pray that you may enjoy good health
and that all may go well with you.
3 John 1:2

December 27

Mercy, peace and love be yours in abundance.
Jude 1:2

December 28

To him who is able to keep you from stumbling
and to present you before his glorious presence
without fault and with great joy—
to the only God our Savior
be glory, majesty, power and authority,
through Jesus Christ our Lord,
before all ages, now and forevermore! Amen.
Jude 1:24–25

December 29

Here I am! I stand at the door and knock.
If anyone hears my voice and opens the door,
I will come in and eat with that person, and they with me.
Revelation 3:20

December 30

"Holy, holy, holy is the Lord God Almighty,"
who was, and is, and is to come.
Revelation 4:8

_____
_____
_____
_____

December 31

I am the Alpha and the Omega,
the First and the Last, the Beginning
and the End.
Revelation 22:13

_____
_____
_____
_____

About the Author

As a speaker, teacher, and author, Tena's passion is to encourage women to grow in faith, hope, and love. She and her family make their home in Illinois. To learn more about Tena's speaking and writing, visit tenadegraaf.com.

Printed in the United States
By Bookmasters